THE ESSENTIAL COLLECTION

ELGAR

GOLD

Published by:
Chester Music
257 Park Avenue South, New York, NY 10010, United States of America.

Exclusive Distributors:
Music Sales Corporation,
257 Park Avenue South, New York, NY 10010, United States of America.
Music Sales Limited,
Distribution Centre, Newmarket Road, Bury St Edmunds, Suffolk IP33 3YB, England.
Music Sales Pty Limited,
120 Rothschild Avenue, Rosebery, NSW 2018, Australia.

Order No. CH71709
ISBN 1-84609-699-5
This book © Copyright 2006 by Chester Music.

Edited by Heather Slater.
Arranging and engraving supplied by Camden Music.
New arrangements by Jerry Lanning.

Printed in the United States of America.

T0056441

CHESTER MUSIC
part of the Music Sales Group
London/New York/Nashville/Los Angeles/Paris/Sydney/Copenhagen/Berlin/Madrid/Tokyo

Edward Elgar

Edward William Elgar was born on 2 June 1857, the fourth son of a Worcestershire piano tuner. Although Edward was surrounded by music it is still a remarkable fact that this most accomplished of English composers was totally self-taught.

During his early life, however, Elgar struggled to gain recognition as a composer and earned money by teaching, playing the violin and directing various local ensembles. In 1886 he met Caroline Alice Roberts whom he married three years later, although Alice's family were opposed to the match, considering music a lowly occupation for a future husband. As an engagement present for Alice, Elgar composed *Salut d'amour*, which, although an early piece, demonstrates Elgar's gift for lyricism. As his compositional style matured with works such as the *Serenade in E Minor* and the *Imperial March* (written for Queen Victoria's Diamond Jubilee) his reputation spread further.

Elgar's breakthrough came in 1899 with his *Enigma Variations*. This work cemented the composer's reputation both nationally and in Europe. The work consists of a theme and fourteen variations, each of these being a musical portrait of one of Elgar's close companions. The most famous is *Nimrod*, which describes the composer's friend and supporter A.J. Jaeger. The name of the work stems from comments Elgar made about a secret countersubject to the main theme, which runs throughout the work but is never made explicit. Scholars have tried to reveal this theme but all have failed. Elgar took the secret to his grave and some have surmised that the whole thing was a joke on the composer's part.

The next few years in Elgar's life would bring a string of lasting and memorable works, including the *Sea Pictures* for contralto and orchestra (two of which appear in this book), the religious oratorio *The Dream Of Gerontius*, and the two short pieces for violin and piano, *Chanson de matin* and *Chanson de nuit*. Whilst Elgar probably regarded the last two of these as little more than a way to earn money, there is no doubt that *The Dream Of Gerontius* was of great personal significance to him. The first performance was a disaster, but a German choirmaster, Julius Buths, was in the audience and recognized the work's merits. He arranged a further performance in Germany and this ensured greater recognition for Elgar.

Between 1901 and 1908, Elgar continued to compose steadily, including the *Pomp And Circumstance Marches Nos. 1–4*. The first of these is more famous as *Land Of Hope And Glory*, although Elgar had no interest in setting such overtly nationalistic words to his music—it was reputedly the idea of King Edward VII. The overtures *Cockaigne* and *In The South* also date from this period. Both pieces have a detailed program and contrast very lively opening sections with sweeping lyrical passages.

Cockaigne concerns a mythical depiction of London, but is also inspired by Elgar's love of nature and the Malvern Hills. *In The South* reflects the composer's love of the Italian countryside, and came about after the Elgars took a holiday to Alassio. The Italian flavor is firmly established when Elgar quotes a Neapolitan song in the best-known section of the work, the *Canto Popolare*. By 1904 Elgar's star was in the firmament—he was knighted and a festival of his music was held in Covent Garden.

Elgar continued to write sacred works, including an oratorio, *The Apostles*, completed in 1903. Although not as famous as *The Dream Of Gerontius*, it contains fine music and shows Wagner's influence upon his work. During this period Elgar also composed two short orchestral pieces that he called *Dream Children*. It has been speculated that these fragments may have come from an abandoned early symphony and were too good to waste. Certainly, along with the *Wand Of Youth* suites, they capture a nostalgic yearning for lost youth.

Elgar first considered writing a symphony as far back as 1898, but another 10 years would pass before he began work in earnest. The first performance of the *Symphony No.1* in 1908 was a great success and it received many subsequent performances. The stately opening adagio theme recurs throughout the work before being transformed into a final triumphant march.

The *Symphony No.2* was completed in 1911 and dedicated to the memory of King Edward, who died in 1910. It was not a success, as Elgar's style had changed—the symphony is full of strongly contrasted emotions and introspective brooding. Such melancholic sentiment is also evident in the *Elegy for Strings*, probably written in response to the death of Elgar's close friend August Jaeger in 1909. The *Violin Concerto*, also written during this time, shows the influence of Brahms and was dedicated to the virtuoso violinist Fritz Kreisler, who gave the premiere performance.

Elgar was deeply affected by the First World War. Of the few pieces he completed in this period, the three settings of war poems that make up *The Spirit Of England* are the most heartfelt and personal. It wasn't until 1918 that he found a final burst of creative energy and completed some fine chamber works and the famous *Cello Concerto*.

It was only a short while after this fertile period that his wife, Alice, died. She had been the inspiration behind his creativity and after she died he wrote little of significance, although at his own death in 1934 he left sketches for an opera, a third symphony (several decades later to be 'elaborated' by composer Anthony Payne) and a piano concerto, hinting at what might have been.

Michael Ahmad, August 2006

Angel's Farewell

(from 'The Dream Of Gerontius', Op.38)

Composed by Edward Elgar

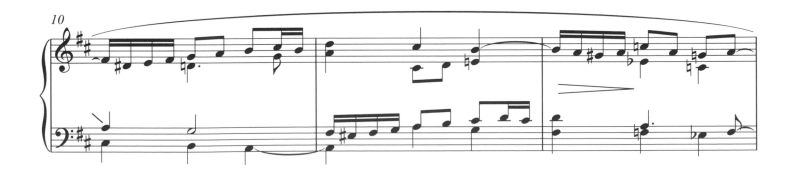

Canto Popolare

(from 'In The South', Op.50)

Composed by Edward Elgar

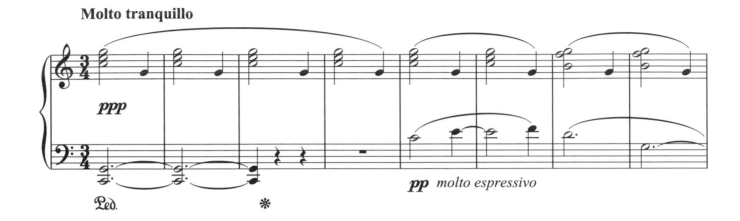

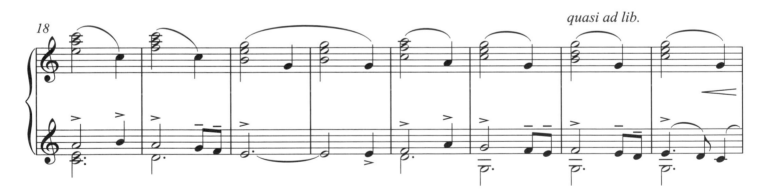

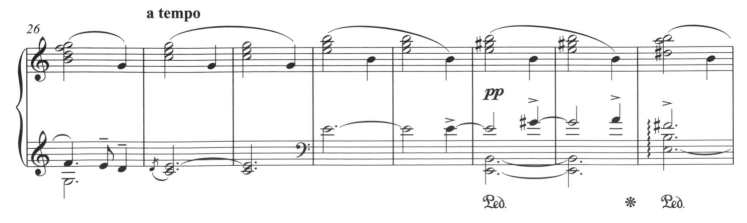

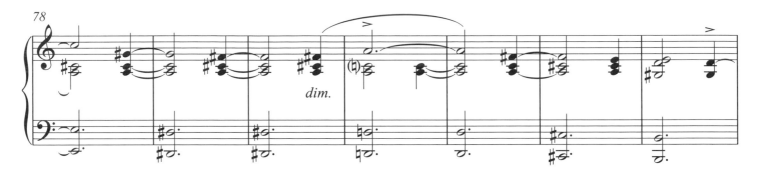

Chanson de nuit, Op.15, No.1

Composed by Edward Elgar

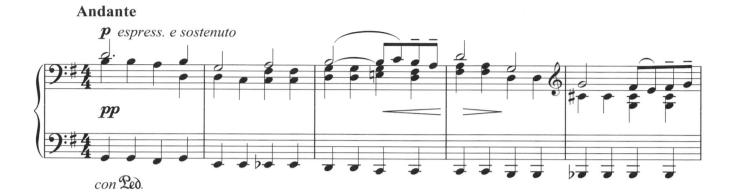

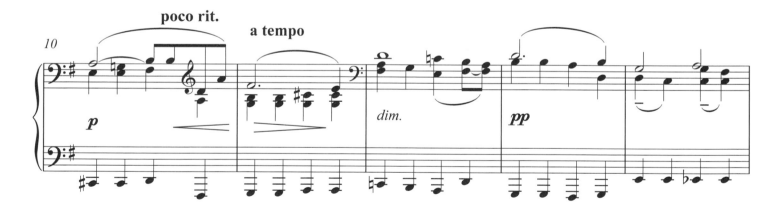

poco stringendo

rall.

Tempo I

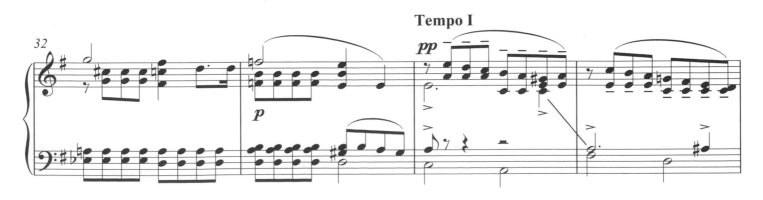

Chanson de matin, Op.15, No.2

Composed by Edward Elgar

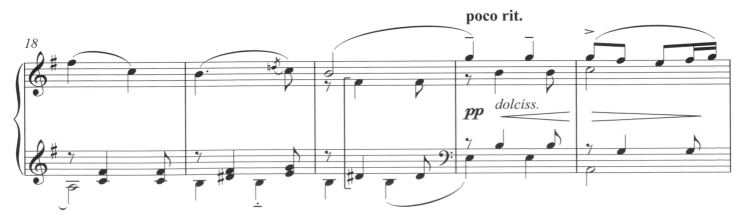

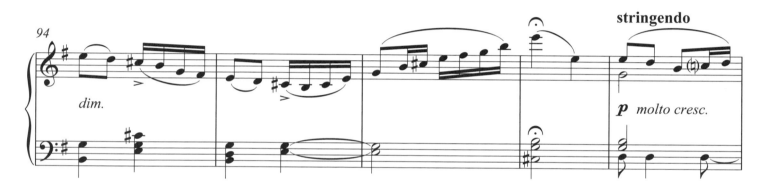

Cockaigne Overture, Op.40

(2nd subject)

Composed by Edward Elgar

Cello Concerto, Op.85

(1st movement)

Composed by Edward Elgar

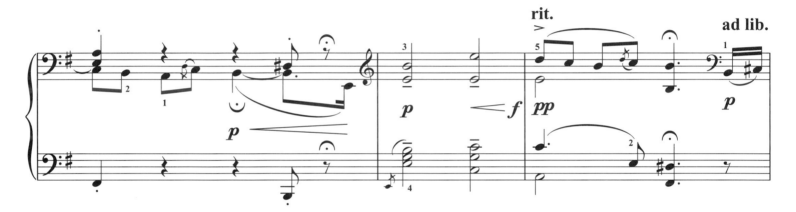

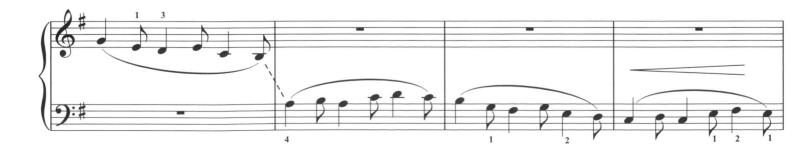

poco allargando

Dream Children, Op.43

(Allegretto piacevole)

Composed by Edward Elgar

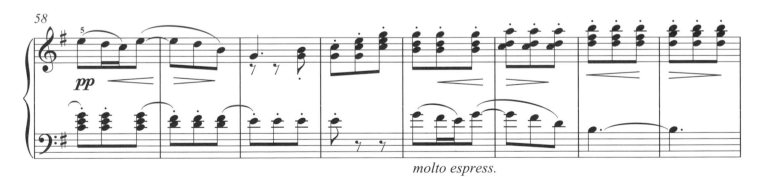

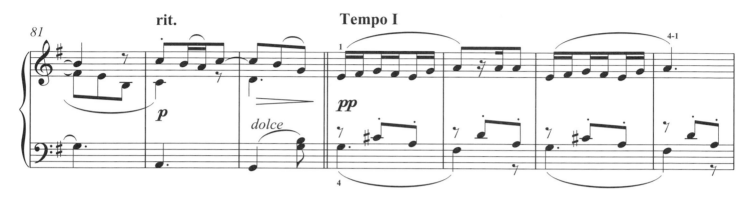

Enigma Variations, Op.36

(Theme)

Composed by Edward Elgar

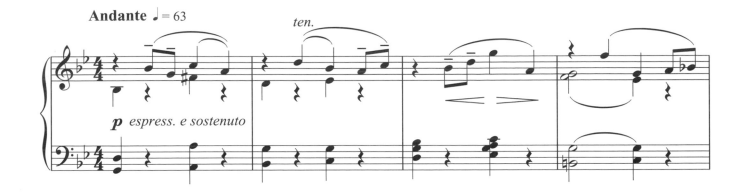

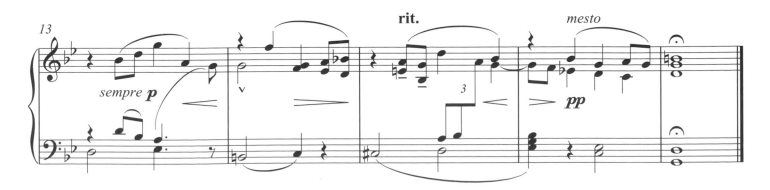

For The Fallen

(from 'The Spirit Of England', Op.80)

Composed by Edward Elgar

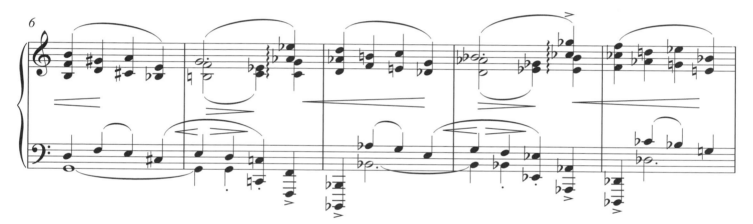

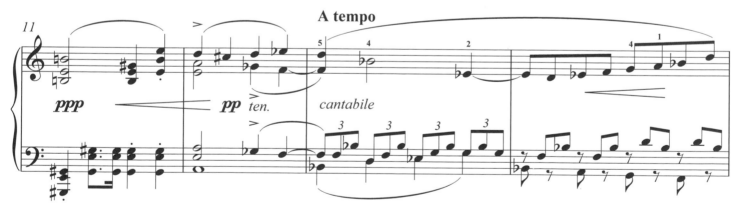

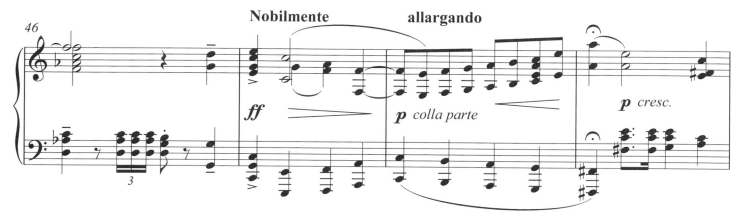

Elegy for Strings, Op.58

Composed by Edward Elgar

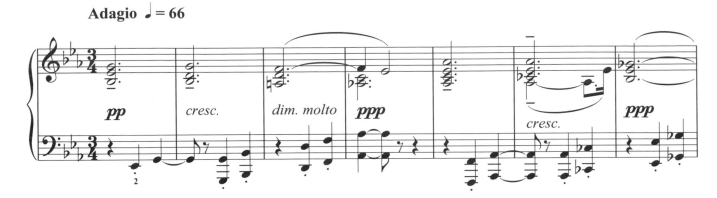

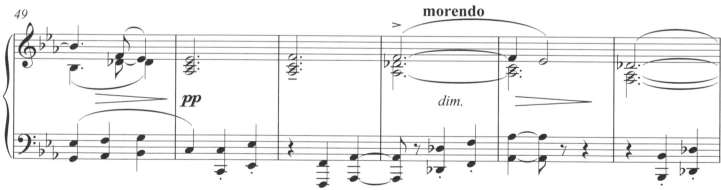

Imperial March, Op.32

Composed by Edward Elgar

Pomposo ♩ = 84

largamente

animato

allargando

poco rit.

poco meno mosso
dolce

largamente

animato

allargando

37

The Music Makers, Op.69

(Introduction)

Composed by Edward Elgar

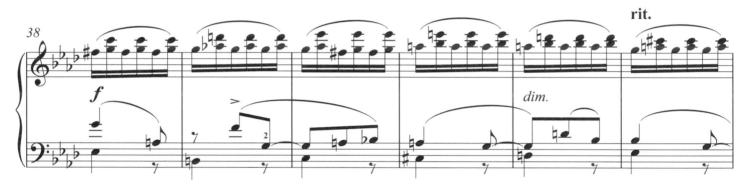

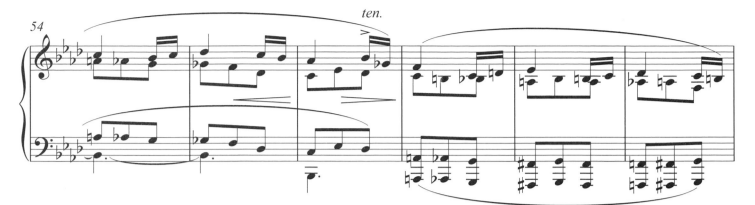

Più tranquillo

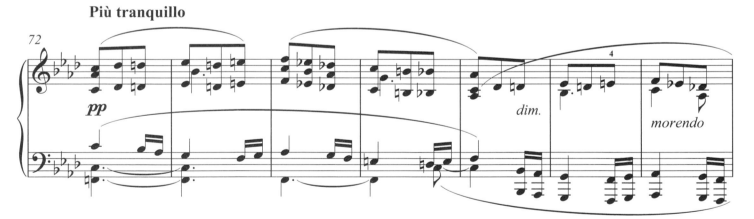

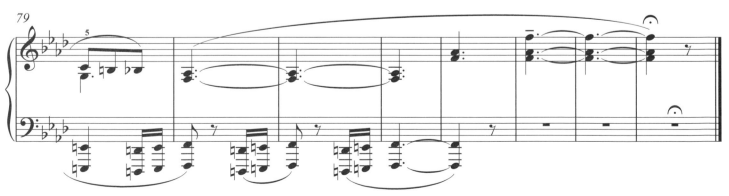

Introduction and Allegro, Op.47

Composed by Edward Elgar

Moderato (♩ = c.80)

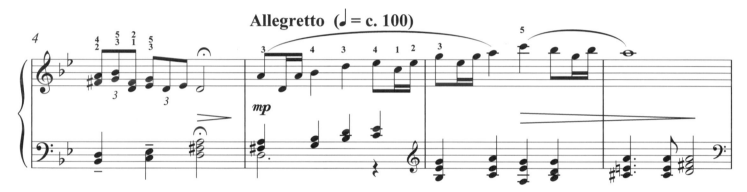

Moderato

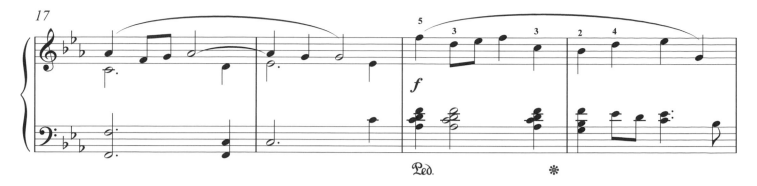

Nimrod

(from 'Enigma Variations', Op.36)

Composed by Edward Elgar

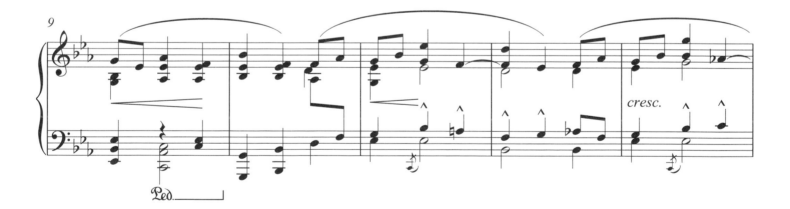

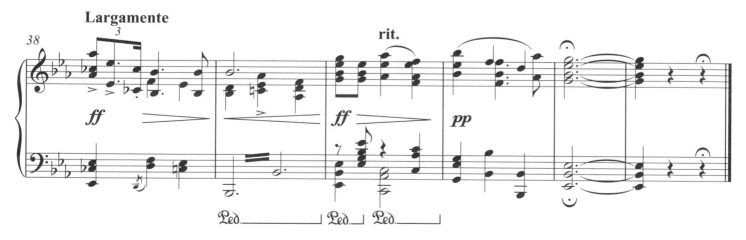

Pomp and Circumstance March No.1

('Land Of Hope And Glory')

Composed by Edward Elgar

Allegro con molto fuoco ♩ = 116

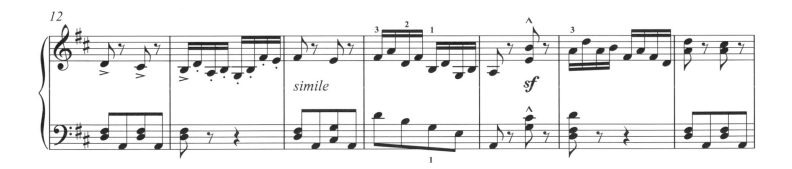

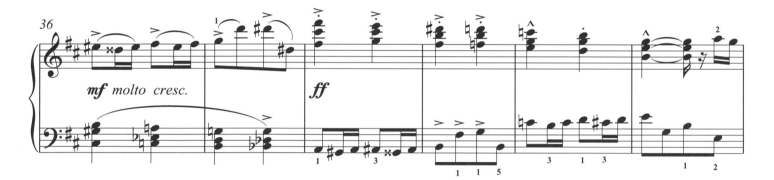

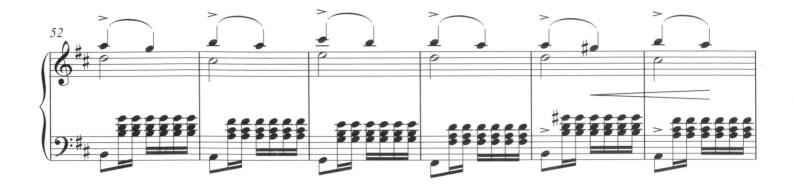

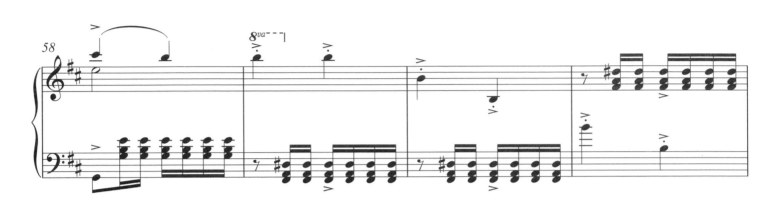

allargando

Pomp and Circumstance March No.4

(Trio)

Composed by Edward Elgar

Piano Quintet, Op.84

(1st movement)

Composed by Edward Elgar

Moderato ♩ = 76

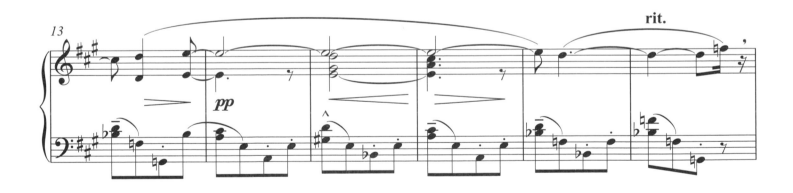

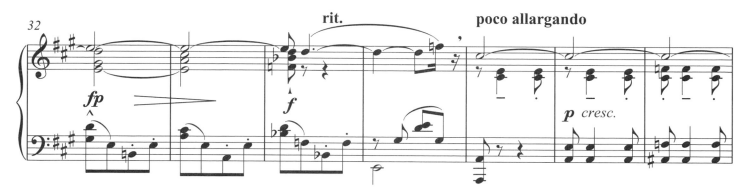

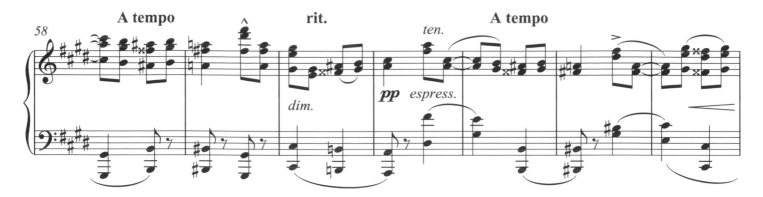

Salut d'amour, Op.12

Composed by Edward Elgar

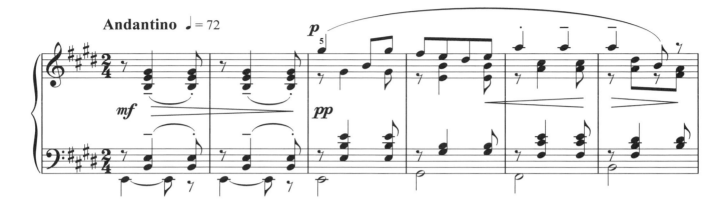

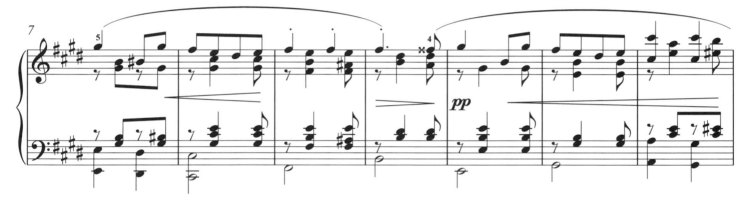

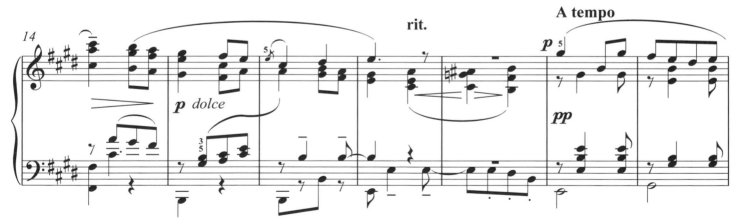

Sea Pictures, Op.37, No.4
'Where Corals Lie'
Composed by Edward Elgar

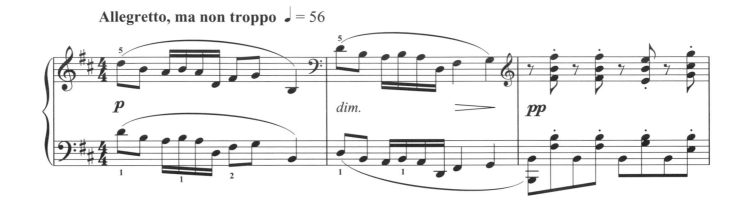

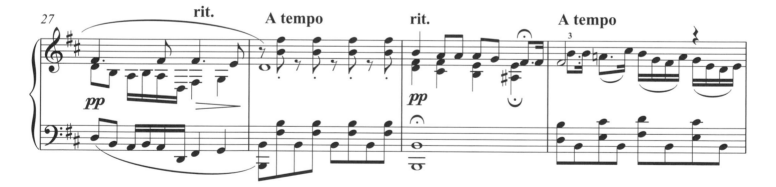

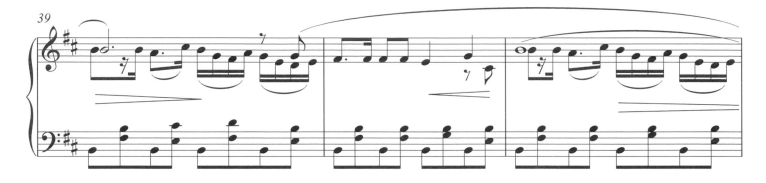

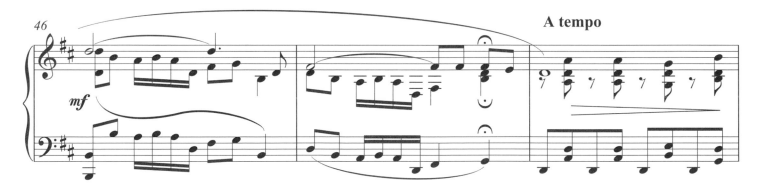

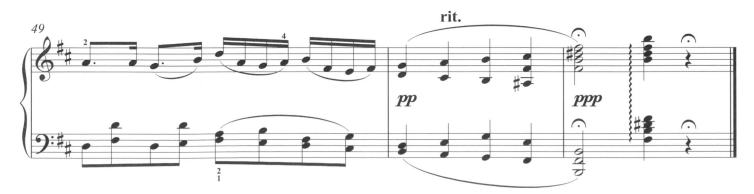

Sea Pictures, Op.37, No.5

'The Swimmer'

Composed by Edward Elgar

allargando

A tempo

poco rall.

rit.

A tempo

Poco meno mosso

62

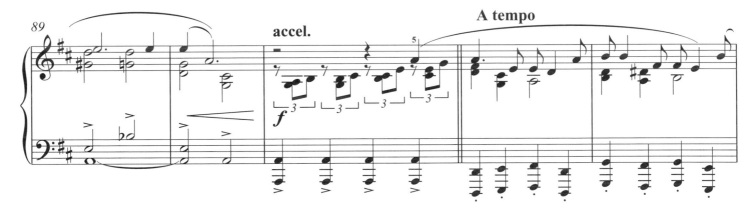

Serenade

(from 'The Wand Of Youth' Suite No.1, Op.1a)

Composed by Edward Elgar

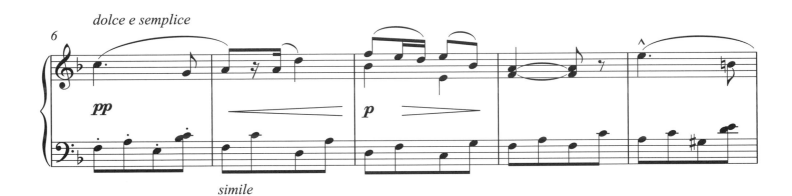

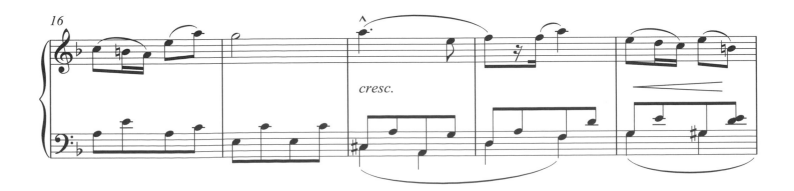

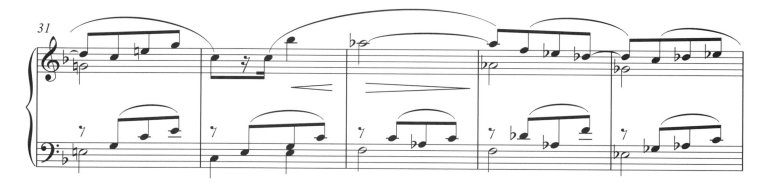

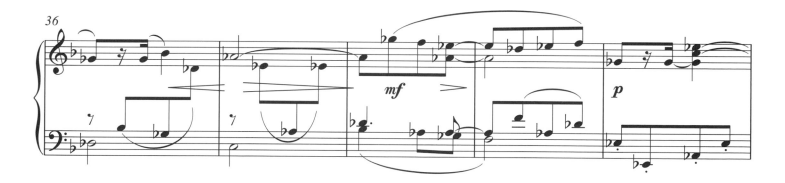

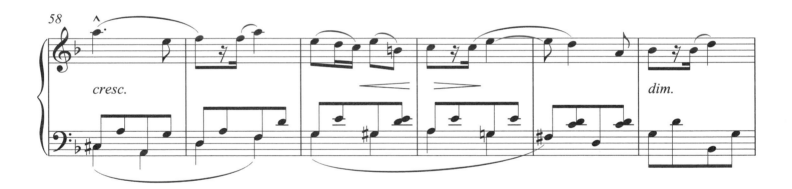

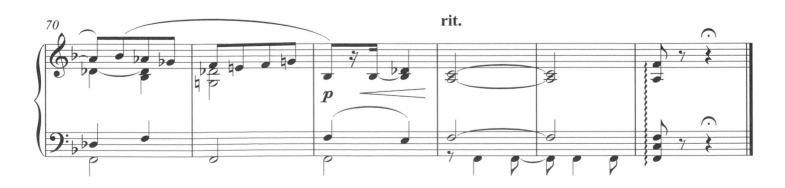

String Quartet in E Minor, Op.83

(2nd movement)

Composed by Edward Elgar

Piacevole (poco andante) ♪ = 104

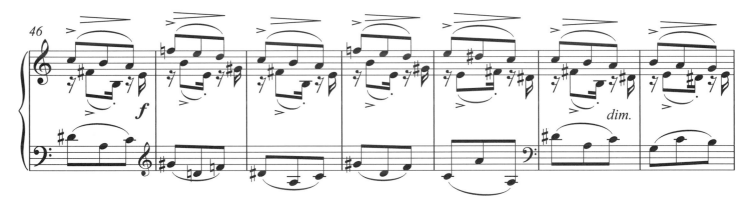

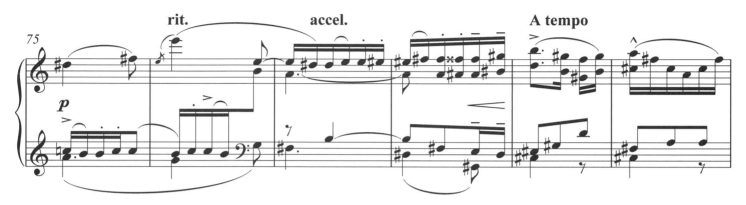

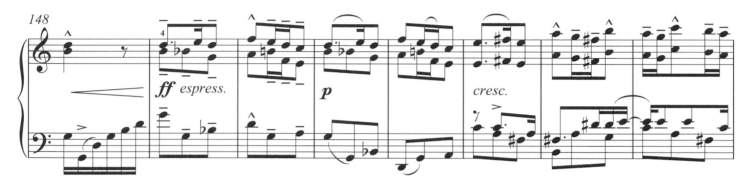

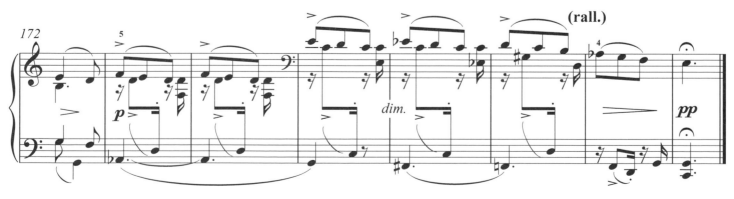

The Spirit Of The Lord Is Upon Me

(Prologue to 'The Apostles', Op.49)

Composed by Edward Elgar

poco animato

poco rall.

poco rit.   A tempo   poco a poco rit.

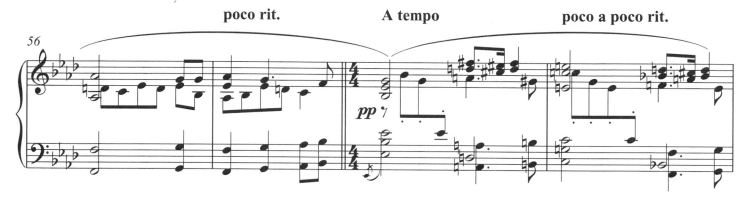

Tempo I

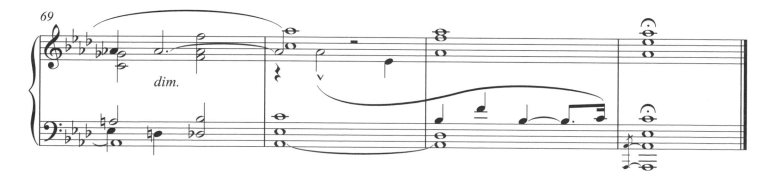

Symphony No.1, Op.55

(Opening theme)

Composed by Edward Elgar

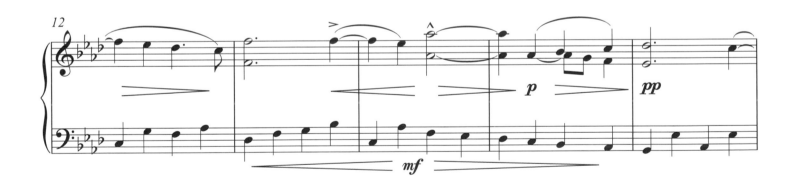

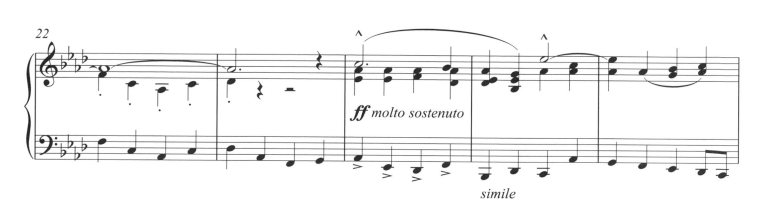

To The Children

(from 'The Starlight Express', Op.78)

Composed by Edward Elgar

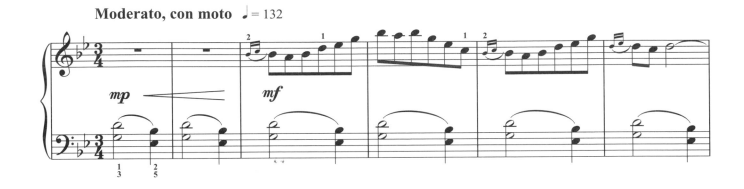

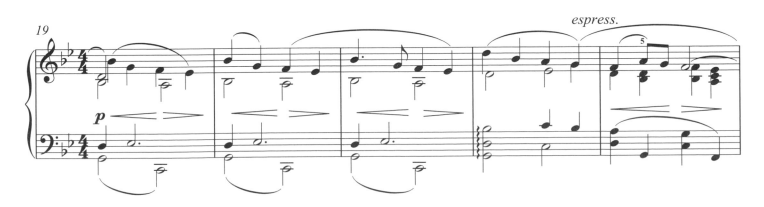

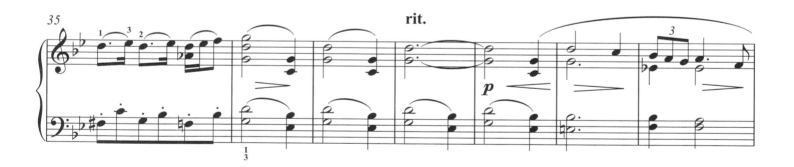

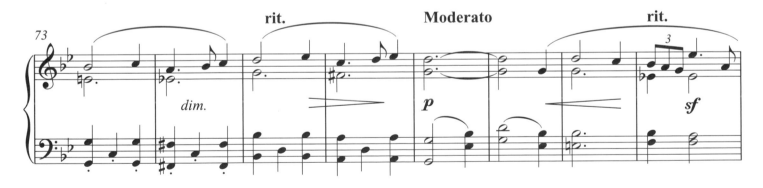

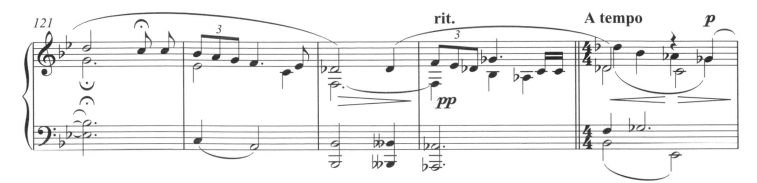

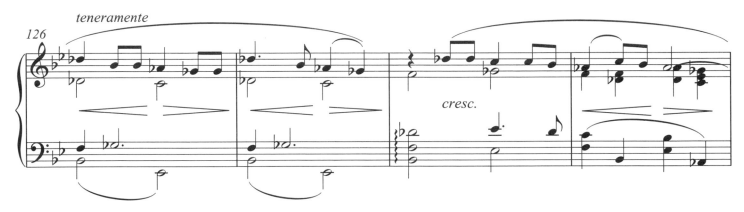

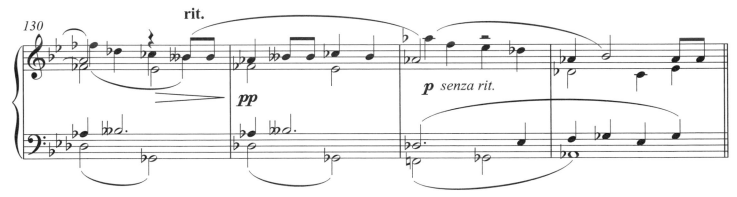

Symphony No.2, Op.63

(2nd movement)

Composed by Edward Elgar

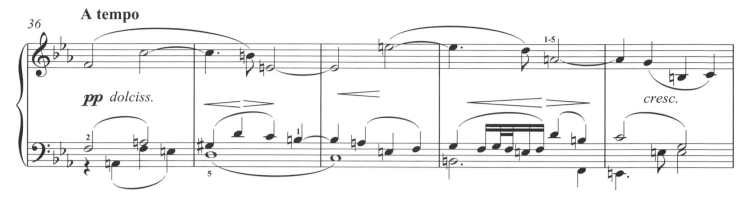

Symphony No.2, Op.63

(Finale)

Composed by Edward Elgar

Moderato e maestoso ♩ = 72

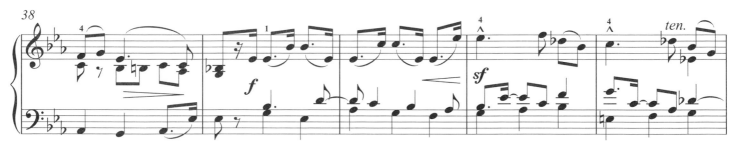

Grandioso

Nobilmente

Violin Concerto, Op.61

(1st movement)

Composed by Edward Elgar

poco allargando   **A tempo**

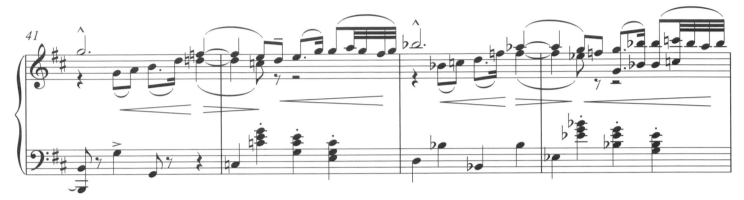

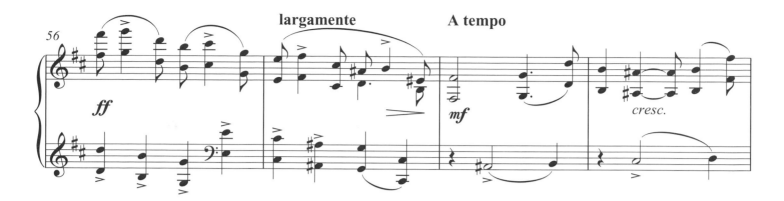

Also available in *The Gold Series*

these beautifully presented albums containing the most famous masterpieces from the world's greatest composers.

BACH GOLD
Includes: Air On A G String,
Aria, Gavotte and Sleepers, Wake!
Order No. CH67067

BEETHOVEN GOLD
Includes: Symphony No.5,
Für Elise, Minuet in G and the
'Moonlight' Sonata.
Order No. CH65670

CHOPIN GOLD
Includes: All famous waltzes, nocturnes,
preludes and mazurkas as well as
excerpts from Piano Concerto No.1
and Sonata No.2 in B♭ Minor.
Order No. CH65681

HANDEL GOLD
Includes: Air (from Water Music),
The Arrival Of The Queen Of Sheba, and
Zadok The Priest (Coronation Anthem)
Order No. CH66792

MOZART GOLD
Includes: A Musical Joke,
Piano Concerto No.21 'Elvira Madigan',
Serenade in B♭ 'Gran Partita' and
Symphony No.40 in G minor.
Order No. CH65505

SCHUMANN GOLD
Includes: music from Album For The
Young, Forest Scenes and Night Pieces.
Order No. CH66863

TCHAIKOVSKY GOLD
Includes: 1812 Overture,
plus music from The Nutcracker,
Sleeping Beauty and
Swan Lake.
Order No. CH65692

*For more information on these and the thousands of
other titles available from Amsco Publications and Chester Music, please contact
www.musicroom.com*